T 18670

DATE DUE

The Pequot Tribe

by Allison Lassieur

Consultant:
James A. Cunha, Jr.
Tribal Chief
Paucatuck Eastern Pequot Indian Tribal Nation

Bridgestone Books
an imprint of Capstone Press
Mankato, Minnesota

Bridgestone Books are published by Capstone Press
151 Good Counsel Drive, P.O. Box 669, Mankato, Minnesota 56002
http://www.capstone-press.com

Library of Congress Cataloging-in-Publication Data
Lassieur, Allison.
The Pequot tribe/by Allison Lassieur.
    p. cm.—(Native peoples)
    Includes bibliographical references and index.
    ISBN 0-7368-0948-1
1. Pequot Indians—Juvenile literature. [1. Pequot Indians. 2. Indians of North America—Connecticut.] I. Title. II. Series.
E99.P53 L37 2002
974'.004973—dc21   00-012602

Summary: An overview of the Pequot, including their history, the Pequot War, homes, food, clothing, religion, and government.

Editorial Credits
Rebecca Glaser, editor; Karen Risch, product planning editor; Timothy Halldin, cover
    designer; Heidi Meyer, illustrator; Jeff Anderson and Deirdre Barton, photo researchers

Photo Credits
Chief James A. Cunha, Jr., 16, 20
Jack McConnell, 12, 14
Marilyn "Angel" Wynn, 6
Mashantucket Pequot Museum and Research Center, cover
North Wind Picture Archives, 8, 10
Photo Network/Bill Terry, 18

Bridgestone Books thanks staff members at the Mashantucket Pequot Museum and Research Center for their assistance with this book.

1 2 3 4 5 6 07 06 05 04 03 02

Table of Contents

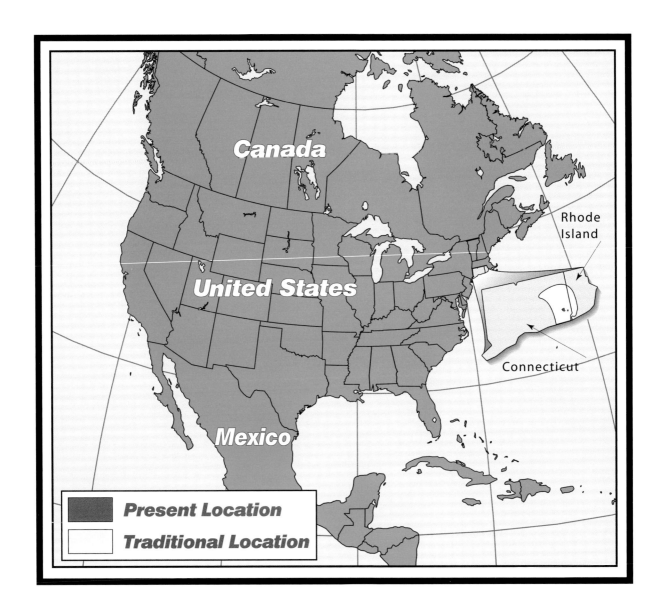

In the past, the Pequots lived in what is now eastern Connecticut and western Rhode Island. Today, several Pequot tribes live on reservations in Connecticut.

Fast Facts

The Pequots were one of the most powerful tribes in the northeastern United States. Today, they still live on the lands of their ancestors. The Pequots' history is important to them. These facts tell about Pequot history.

Homes: The Pequots lived in wigwams. These homes were made of young trees called saplings. The wigwams' frames were covered with bark or mats.

Food: Pequot men and boys hunted deer and other wild animals for food. The women and girls planted crops of corn, beans, and squash. They also caught fish and shellfish from rivers and from the ocean.

Clothing: The Pequots wore clothing made from animal skins. Men had breechcloths and leggings. Women dressed in short or long skirts, depending on the season. In the winter, Pequots wore warm wraps made from animal furs.

Language: The Pequot language is an Eastern Algonquian language. Many tribes in the northeastern United States and southeastern Canada spoke languages in this group.

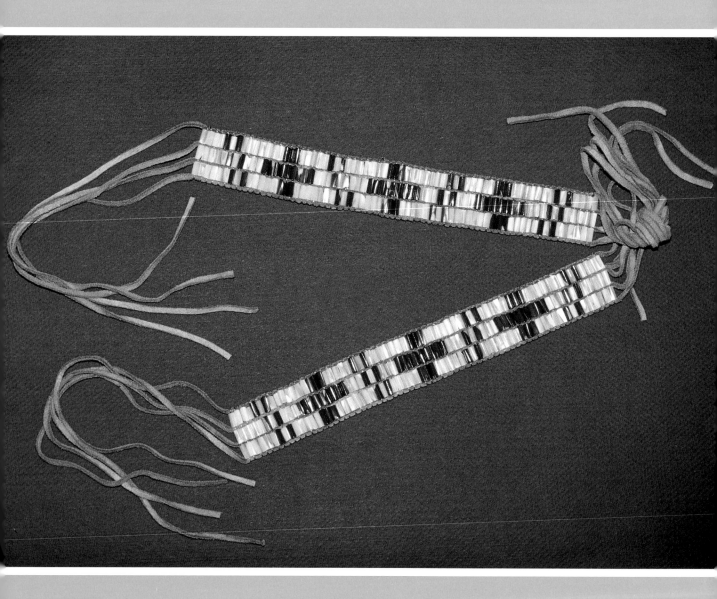

American Indians used the purple shells of the quahog clam to make wampum. They strung wampum together to make belts.

Early Pequot History

The Pequots have always lived near shallow rivers in what is now Connecticut. The word "Pequot" means "people of the shallow waters."

In the early 1600s, Dutch traders came to the area. They built trading posts. The Dutch traded with many tribes, including the Pequots. The Pequots and other tribes along the coast traded furs and wampum for European items.

The English also settled in the area. They wanted to trade with the same tribes. The competition for trade caused conflicts and some fighting. The English also fought with the Dutch over trade.

Wampum was an important part of the fur trade. American Indians first made these strings of shell beads for tribal ceremonies. American Indians gave wampum to other tribes as a sign of friendship. Europeans used wampum like money to buy furs and other trade items from American Indians.

The Pequot War

In 1636, an Englishman named John Oldham was killed. The Pequots did not kill him. But they were blamed for his death. English colonists sent soldiers to attack the Pequots. This surprise attack was the first battle of the Pequot War.

The English and the Pequots fought many battles. The Pequots asked the Narragansett tribe to help them fight the English. The Narragansetts refused. The Narragansetts joined the Mohegan tribe to help the English instead. They helped the English find a Pequot village. Today this village is called Mystic Fort.

The English attacked the village in 1637. More than 600 Pequots died. The English continued to attack the Pequots in the summer of 1637. The war ended in 1638 when the Treaty of Hartford was signed.

More than 600 Pequots died when the English attacked Mystic Fort in 1637.

After the Pequot War

Many Pequots survived the war. But the English wanted to destroy the Pequot way of life. They made it illegal to say the word "Pequot."

The English sent some Pequots to Bermuda as slaves. They gave another group to the Mohegan tribe. A third group went to the Narragansett tribe. Some Pequots became household servants for the English. Other Pequots escaped. But the English made it illegal for other tribes to help the Pequots.

The Pequots did not live with the other tribes forever. The English colonists finally allowed the Pequots to leave the Mohegans and Narragansetts. Each group of Pequots lived on separate parts of their old lands. The Pequots became two tribes, the Mashantucket Pequots and the Paucatuck Pequots.

The English forced Pequots to move to different places after the war.

The Pequot Today

In the late 1600s, the Connecticut colony set aside land, called reservations, for the Pequot tribes. Over the years, many Pequots died in wars. Some Pequots moved off the reservations to find work. But the two tribes continued to exist. They dreamed of bringing all Pequots back to the reservation.

In 1983, the U.S. Congress passed a law that recognized the Mashantucket Pequots as a tribe. It also settled a land claim. The law gave money to the tribe to create jobs and buy land.

In 1992, the Mashantucket Pequots opened Foxwoods Casino. Today, they are one of the most successful tribes in the United States. In 1998, they opened a research center where people can find out about the histories of all tribes.

The Paucatuck Pequots are applying for federal recognition from the U.S. government. With recognition, the tribe would receive help from government programs.

The Mashantucket Pequots opened Foxwoods Casino on their reservation in 1992.

Homes, Food, and Clothing

The Pequots' traditional home was a wigwam. A wigwam had a dome-shaped wooden frame. The Pequots covered the frame with bark or mats of woven plants. The Pequots moved with the seasons. They had a wigwam frame at each place. A family covered the frame with the mats. When they left, they took their mats with them.

The Pequots' food came from many sources. Pequot men hunted deer and other wild animals. Women gathered wild plants, nuts, and berries from the forest. The Pequots moved to the coast in the summer. Men fished the rivers and the ocean for fish, shellfish, and other animals. Women planted crops of corn, beans, and squash.

The Pequots traditionally wore clothes made from animal skins such as deerskin. Men dressed in breechcloths and leggings. Women wore skirts. In the winter, the Pequots wrapped themselves in warm animal furs.

This display at the Mashantucket Pequot Museum and Research Center shows a traditional Pequot wigwam.

Pequot Religion

The Pequots believed that people must treat Earth and everything on it with respect. Every living thing in the world has a spirit. One Great Spirit oversees everything.

After the Pequot War, many people stopped worshipping in traditional ways. But some Pequots still followed the traditional beliefs.

Today, many Pequot children learn about the spirits of living creatures. They learn that it is wrong to kill for no reason. Hunters who kill animals for food must make an offering to the animal's spirit. The offering thanks the spirit for the food.

Today, most Pequots follow other religions such as Christianity. They also keep some of their traditional beliefs. Every year the Pequots hold a powwow. They perform dances that show how the Pequots prayed to the Great Spirit. Tribal elders teach others about the Pequots' traditions and beliefs.

Paucatuck Pequot council members gathered at the 7th Annual Paucatuck Eastern Pequot Harvest Moon Powwow.

The Women and the Sea

Long ago, the Pequots did not write down their legends and stories. But some legends from Connecticut tribes have survived in books written by European settlers.

One story is about two beautiful women. One day they went swimming in the ocean. The white foam of the ocean waves touched the women. They became pregnant. One woman had a baby boy. The other woman had a baby girl. The two women then died and left Earth. The boy and the girl grew up. They became the parents of all the people in the world.

The Paucatuck Pequots also believe that the world was created on the back of a turtle. They say that their tribe is like the turtle. They are both small and slow moving, but they will survive.

One American Indian story tells how the ocean helped create the parents of all the people in the world.

Pequot Government

Long ago, leaders called sachems (SAY-chems) led the Pequot tribe. Sachem means leader in the Pequot language. The tribe also had a council of elders. They talked about relationships with other tribes, crops, hunting, and other subjects.

Today, each of the Pequot tribes has a tribal council. The tribes elect the members of their councils in different ways. Each council has different rules for running its tribe.

For example, nine people are members of the Paucatuck Pequot council. Four of them are elders from Pequot families. The elders are on the council for life. The people elect the other five members. The council is in charge of day-to-day life in the tribe. The Grand Chief Sachem is a spiritual leader. He and the other elders are responsible for religion and culture.

Atwood Williams also was known as Silver Star, Chief Sachem. He led the Paucatuck Pequots and the Mashantucket Pequots in the 1920s and 1930s.

Hands On: Make Shell Jewelry

The Pequots wore a lot of jewelry. They made necklaces and bracelets from shells they found along the coast. Some types of shells were a sign of wealth and respect to the Pequot people. You can make your own shell jewelry.

What You Need

Small shells
Scissors
Leather or plastic string
Craft glue

What You Do

1. Choose some shells and wash them thoroughly. Let them dry.
2. Cut the leather or plastic string to the length that you want the necklace to be.
3. Put a drop of glue on the end of a shell and glue it to the string.
4. Continue gluing shells until the string is filled. Let the glue dry.
5. Tie the ends of the string together to make a necklace.

Words to Know

ancestor (AN-sess-tur)—a member of a family who lived a long time ago, such as a great-grandparent

breechcloth (BREECH-kloth)—a piece of deerskin clothing that hangs from the waist and passes between the legs

Christianity (kriss-chee-AN-uh-tee)—a religion based on the life and teachings of Jesus Christ

colonist (KOL-uh-nist)—a person living in a newly settled area

council (KOUN-suhl)—a group of leaders

religion (ri-LIJ-uhn)—a set of spiritual beliefs that people follow

tradition (truh-DISH-uhn)—a custom, idea, or belief that is passed down from one generation to the next

Read More

Ansary, Mir Tamim. *Eastern Woodlands Indians.* Native Americans. Chicago: Heinemann Library, 2000.

Newman, Shirlee P. *The Pequots.* Watts Library. New York: Franklin Watts, 2000.

Sita, Lisa. *Indians of the Northeast: Traditions, History, Legends, and Life.* Native Americans. Milwaukee: Gareth Stevens, 2000.

Useful Addresses

**Mashantucket Pequot
   Museum and Research
   Center**
110 Pequot Trail
P.O. Box 3180
Mashantucket, CT 06339-3180

**Paucatuck Eastern Pequot
Indian Tribal Nation**
P.O. Box 370
North Stonington, CT 06359

Internet Sites

Mashantucket Pequot Museum and Research Center
http://www.mashantucket.com
Native Tech
http://www.nativetech.org
Paucatuck Eastern Pequot Indian Tribal Nation
http://www.paucatuck.org

Index